GN00371879

ínspirations

STENCILLING

20 decorative projects for the home

inspirations

STENCILLING

20 decorative projects for the home

SACHA COHEN

PHOTOGRAPHY BY ADRIAN TAYLOR

LORENZ BOOKS

LONDON • NEW YORK • SYDNEY • BATH

This edition published in the UK in 1997 by Lorenz Books

Lorenz Books is an imprint of Anness Publishing Limited
Hermes House
88-89 Blackfriars Road
London SE1 8HA

This edition published in Canada by Lorenz Books, distributed by
Raincoast Books Distribution Limited, Vancouver

© Anness Publishing Limited 1997

ISBN 1 85967 429 1

All rights reserved. No part of this publication may be reproduced, stored in a retrieval system or transmitted in any way or
by any means, electronic, mechanical, photocopying, recording or otherwise without the prior written
permission of the copyright holder.

A CIP catalogue record for this book is available from the British Library

Publisher: Joanna Lorenz
Senior Editor: Lindsay Porter
Designer: Bobbie Colgate Stone
Photographer: Adrian Taylor
Illustrators: Madeleine David and Lucinda Ganderton

Printed and bound in Hong Kong

1 3 5 7 9 10 8 6 4 2

CONTENTS

INTRODUCTION

Stencilling was the first paint effect that I ever tried and I remember being amazed at how quick and easy it was. Stencilling has been used in interior design for centuries, either to add delicate decoration to a grand scheme, or as an alternative to expensive wallpapers. Today we are witnessing a revival in the art of stencilling, with stencils and paints for every surface now widely available.

This book is designed to inspire you to experiment with stencilling, while at the same time adding an individual touch to your home. Stencilling is more than the mere act of adding a splash of colour to an otherwise plain room: it is an art in its own right, and furthermore, one that enables you to create a decorative effect that would be impossible to achieve by any other means. It is a simple, cheap and impressive way of decorating any surface. Stencils are highly adaptable and can be used on items large and small to invest them with character. You will be pleasantly surprised at how little time it takes to transform even the largest surface with a pattern.

This book features clear step-by-step photography to guide you through basic stencilling techniques, before moving on to larger projects for the more experienced craft artist. All the patterns for the stencils are included, together with information on materials required. Every medium is covered, including stencilling on fabrics, floors, walls and glass, as well as special tips for every surface. Designs range from heraldic patterns to seashore motifs. Experiment with colours: you can transform a pattern by using either subtle or bright shades. Finally, a word of warning: once you find out just how easy stencilling can be, it can prove very difficult to stop.

Deborah Barker

FROSTED VASES

Give coloured or clear glass vases the designer touch using glass etching cream and reverse stencilling. The shapes are cut from sticky-backed plastic and removed after stencilling to reveal the clear outlines. Choose flowers and leaves, stripes or spots - the choice is yours. The same technique could be used to transform windows.

YOU WILL NEED
glass vase
sticky-backed plastic
scissors
rubber gloves
glass etching cream
soft paintbrush

1 Wash the vase with hot soapy water to remove any grease. Leave the vase to dry. Trace the flower and leaf templates at the back of the book and transfer them on to the back of a piece of sticky-backed plastic. Cut out the shapes with scissors.

2 Decide where you want to position the shapes on the vase, remove the backing paper and stick in place, smoothing them down.

4 Still wearing the rubber gloves, wash the cream off the vase with warm water and leave to dry. If there are blotchy areas where the cream hasn't worked, simply paint the vase again and leave it for another 30 minutes. When you are happy with the results, peel off the sticky shapes and wash the vase again to remove any sticky smears from the plastic.

3 Wearing rubber gloves, paint the etching cream evenly over the outside of the vase with a paintbrush, and leave to dry in a warm, dust-free area for about 30 minutes.

▶

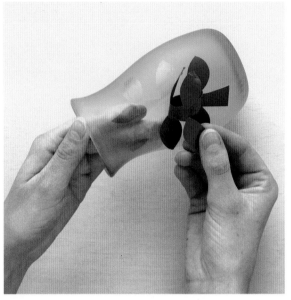

5 For a smaller vase, try using just one motif. Paint on the etching cream in the same way as for the large vase and leave it for 30 minutes.

6 Wash off the etching cream and peel off the plastic motif to reveal the design, then wash the vase again.

7 For a striped frosted vase, cut out straight or wiggly strips of sticky-backed plastic and stick them on to the vase. Paint on the etching cream as before and leave to dry for 30 minutes.

8 Wash off the etching cream, then peel off the plastic strips and wash the vase again to remove any sticky smears from the plastic.

PAINTED DRAWERS

Jazz up plain, unfinished drawers with bright paintbox colours and simple daisy stencils. The same stencils could be used to decorate larger pieces of furniture such as a chest of drawers for a child's room or to update plain kitchen units. Emulsion sample pots are ideal to use on small projects.

YOU WILL NEED
set of wooden drawers
sandpaper
emulsion paints in various colours
paintbrush
screwdriver
acetate
craft knife and cutting mat
stencil brush
matt acrylic varnish
wood glue (optional)

1 Remove the drawers and sand down the frame and drawers to remove any rough areas or patches of old paint.

2 Paint the drawer frame using emulsion paint and a paintbrush. Leave to dry, then apply a second coat of paint.

3 Unscrew the drawer knobs and paint each drawer in a different-coloured emulsion paint. Leave to dry and apply a second coat. Trace the flower template at the back of the book and cut a stencil from acetate as described in the basic techniques.

4 When the drawers are dry, position the flower stencil in the centre of a drawer and, using a stencil brush and paint in a contrasting colour, stencil on the flower. Leave to dry.

5 Stencil a flower in the centre of each drawer, using a different colour for each one.

▶

6 Paint the drawer knobs with two coats of paint, leaving them to dry between coats. Leave to dry.

7 Screw or glue a painted knob to the centre of each drawer. Varnish the drawers with matt acrylic varnish. Leave to dry before reassembling.

ART NOUVEAU HATBOX

An elegantly stencilled hatbox and matching shoe bag would be perfect for storing a bride's hat and shoes. Make a set for yourself or to give to someone special. And you needn't stop there: stencil a whole stack of matching hatboxes to use for stylish storage in a bedroom.

YOU WILL NEED
round hatbox
white undercoat
paintbrushes
water-based woodwash in
pale green
tape measure
pencil
stencil card
craft knife and cutting mat
ruler
spray adhesive
stencil brushes
stencil paints in dark green,
royal blue and pale green

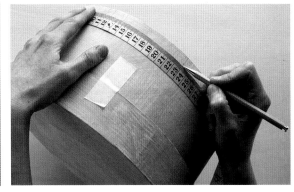

1 Paint the hatbox with two coats of white under-coat. Dilute one part pale green woodwash with one part water and apply two or three light washes to the hatbox, allowing them to dry between coats. Measure the circumference of the box and divide by six or eight. Lightly mark the measurements on the lid and side of the box with a pencil.

2 Trace the flower and heart templates at the back of the book. Cut the stencils from stencil card as described in the basic techniques. Rule a pencil line across the bottom of the stencil to help align it on the box. Spray lightly with adhesive and position on the box. Using a stencil brush and dark green stencil paint, stencil the leaves and stem. Remove the stencil when dry, respray with adhesive and reposition. Continue to work around the box.

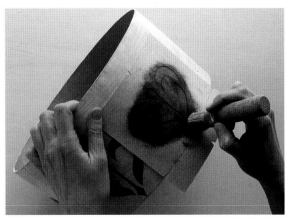

3 Reposition the stencil on the leaves, and add shadow to the points where the leaves join the stem using royal blue paint. Use a clean brush to keep the colours clean.

4 Using the single heart stencil, add a pale green heart between each pair of leaves.

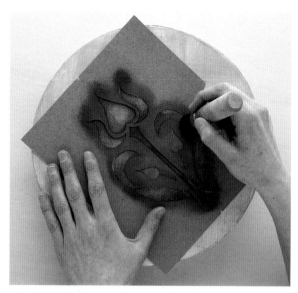

5 Stencil flowerheads around the rim of the lid in dark green, adding a royal blue shadow as before. Stencil the flower motif in the centre of the lid.

6 Add pale green heart motifs around the main motif, using a very small amount of paint for a delicate touch.

Above: Stencil a matching calico shoe bag, using fabric paints, to protect a treasured pair of shoes.

STAR FRAME

Give plain or old picture frames a new look with textured stars. Adding ready-mixed filler to acrylic stencil paint gives a three-dimensional effect to stencilled designs. Once you have mixed your plaster you will need to work quickly before it sets.

YOU WILL NEED
wooden picture frame
emulsion paints in dark and light blue
paintbrush
soft cloth
wax furniture polish
sandpaper
acetate
craft knife and cutting mat
bowl
ready-mixed filler
acrylic paint in dark blue
stencil brush
flowerpots

1 Paint the frame in dark blue emulsion paint using a paintbrush. When dry, apply a second coat and leave to dry.

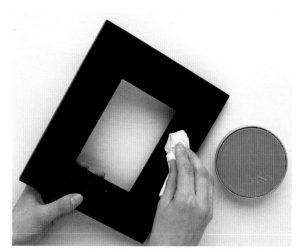

2 Using a soft cloth, rub wax furniture polish all over the frame and leave to dry.

3 Paint the frame with light blue emulsion paint and leave to dry. Paint on a second coat and leave to dry. Then lightly sand the frame to create a distressed effect. ▶

4 Cut a large and a small star stencil from acetate as described in the basic techniques. In a bowl, mix together the ready-mixed filler and acrylic paint until you are happy with the shade, remembering that when the filler dries it will be much lighter.

5 Position the star stencil on the frame and dab on the filler with a stencil brush. Keep stencilling until you have covered the frame. Leave the filler to harden and wash the brush thoroughly.

6 When the filler has dried and hardened, gently smooth the stars with sandpaper.

7 Paint and stencil the flowerpots in the same way as the picture frame.

MAKING SANDCASTLES

Evocative of childhood summers spent on the beach, sandcastles are simple, colourful shapes to stencil. Perfect for a child's room or for a family bathroom, they will bring a touch of humour to your walls. Paint the flags in different colours or glue on paper flags for added interest.

YOU WILL NEED
emulsion paints in blue and white
paintbrush
household sponge
acetate
craft knife and cutting mat
tape measure
pencil
masking tape
stencil paints in yellow, black and other colours of your choice
stencil brushes
fine paintbrush
coloured paper (optional)
PVA glue (optional)

1 Paint below dado-rail height in blue. When dry, rub on white emulsion with a sponge. Trace the templates at the back of the book. Cut the stencils from acetate as described in the basic techniques.

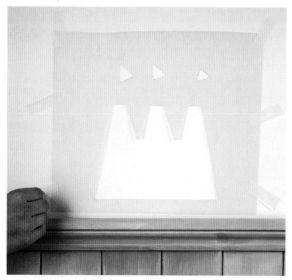

2 Measure the wall to calculate how many sand-castles you can fit on and make light pencil marks at regular intervals. Hold the stencil above the dado rail and secure the corners with masking tape.

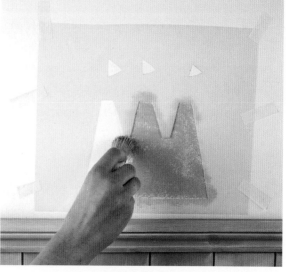

3 Using yellow stencil paint and a stencil brush, stencil in the first sandcastle.

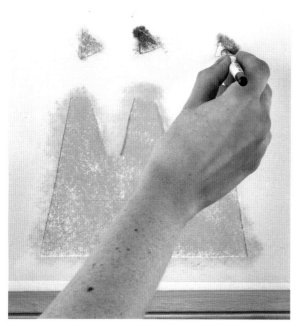

4 Stencil each flag in a different colour and remove the stencil.

5 When the paint has dried, stencil a star on the sandcastle in a contrasting colour of paint.

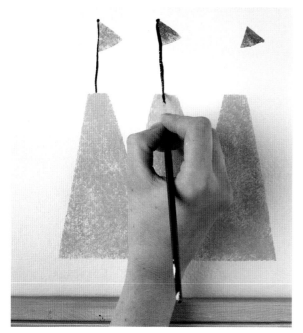

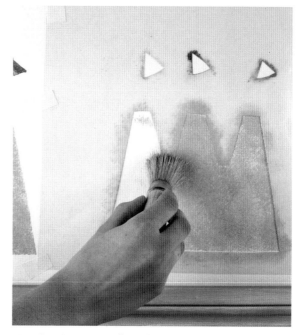

6 Using a fine paintbrush and black stencil paint, paint in the flagpoles.

7 Continue stencilling the sandcastles along the wall using your pencil marks to position them. ▶

8 As an alternative to stencilling the flags, cut out triangles of coloured paper and glue them to the wall with PVA glue, then paint in the flagpoles.

Above: Don't be too exacting when painting the flagpoles. Wobbly lines and erratic angles add to the childlike quality of the sandcastle frieze.

Left: A variation on the seashore theme might include bright tropical shapes in Caribbean colours.

SEASHORE BATHROOM SET

Seaside themes are always popular for a bathroom and these stencils in fresh blue and white link the different elements of the room. For best results, choose paints to suit the surface you are planning to stencil: enamel paint for plastic and glass and fabric paint for the towels.

YOU WILL NEED
acetate
craft knife and cutting mat
clear plastic shower curtain
stencil brush
enamel paints in white and blue
smooth cotton hand towel
fabric paint in dark blue
iron
2 glass tumblers
masking tape (optional)

1 Trace the shell, starfish and fish templates at the back of the book. Cut the stencils from acetate as described in the basic techniques. Lay the shower curtain on a flat surface. Lightly dab the stencil brush in the white enamel paint and begin to stencil the shapes on the curtain.

2 Continue to stencil the shapes randomly over the whole shower curtain, taking care not to overload the brush with paint. Leave to dry.

3 Reposition the stencils on the painted shapes and dab on the blue paint. Leave some of the shapes white. Leave the curtain to dry before hanging in place.

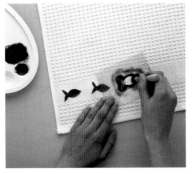

4 Lay the hand towel on a flat surface. Using the fish stencil and dark blue fabric paint, stencil a border of fish across one short edge of the towel.

5 Stencil the opposite edge of the towel, arranging the fish in a different way. Iron the towel to fix the fabric paint, following the manufacturer's instructions. ▶

6 For the glass, hold or tape the fish stencil in place and gently dab on white enamel paint.

7 Leave to dry, then reposition the stencil and continue to stencil fish all over the glass. Decorate the second glass with blue fish. The glasses should only be used for decoration; do not apply enamel paints to surfaces that will be eaten from.

Above: Blue and white stencils work well in a plain white bathroom. You can also choose colours to coordinate with your existing decor.

GREEK URNS

Classic Greek urns softly outlined under a warm terracotta colourwash have a very Mediterranean feel. The stencilling is worked in clear varnish so that the top colour slides over without adhering, leaving subtly coloured motifs. Arrange the urns randomly over the wall for an informal finish.

YOU WILL NEED
emulsion paints in cream and terracotta
large household sponge
acetate
craft knife and cutting mat
masking tape
stencil brush
satin acrylic varnish
wallpaper paste
cloth

1 Working in rough, sweeping strokes, rub a base coat of warm cream emulsion over the wall using a sponge. Trace the urn template at the back of the book and cut a stencil from acetate as described in the basic techniques. Tape it to the wall and stencil with clear acrylic varnish. Reposition the stencil and cover the wall with randomly arranged urns.

2 Make up the wallpaper paste following the pack instructions. Mix one part terracotta emulsion with one part paste. This will make the colourwash slimy and slow down the drying time so as to prevent "joins" in the finished colourwash. Using a sponge, dab lumps of the mixture over about 1 m/3 ft square of the wall.

3 Immediately rub the wall in a circular motion to blur the sponge marks.

▶

4 Continue dabbing on paint and blurring with the sponge to cover the whole wall. The varnished urns should be revealed underneath the colourwash.

5 If the urns are not clear enough, use a slightly damp cloth and your index finger to rub off a little more wash from the varnished shape. This can be done even when the wall has dried or after the room has been completed.

Left: Try colourwashing duck-egg blue over a beige background as an alternative colour combination.

PENNSYLVANIA-DUTCH TULIPS

This American folk-art inspired idea uses the rich colours and simple motifs beloved by the German and Dutch immigrants to Pennsylvania. Create the effect of hand-painted wallpaper or, for a beginner's project, take a single motif and use to decorate a key cupboard.

YOU WILL NEED
emulsion paint in dark ochre
large and small paintbrushes
woodwash in indigo blue and mulberry
stencil card
craft knife and cutting mat
pencil
ruler
stencil brushes
stencil paints in red, light green, dark green and pale brown
saucer or cloth
artist's paintbrush

1 Dilute one part ochre emulsion with one part water. Using a large paintbrush, cover the top half of the wall with the diluted emulsion. Use vertical brush strokes for an even texture.

2 Paint the lower half of the wall with indigo blue woodwash. Finish off with a curving line using a dry brush to suggest woodgrain.

3 Paint the dado rail or a strip at dado-rail height in mulberry woodwash using a narrow brush to give a clean edge.

4 Trace the tulip and heart templates at the back of the book and cut the stencils from stencil card as described in the basic techniques. Mark the centre of each edge of the stencil. Measure the wall and divide it into equal sections, so that the repeats will fall at about 20 cm/8 in intervals. Mark the positions lightly with pencil, so that they can be rubbed out later.

5 Dip the stencil brush into red stencil paint. Rub the brush on a saucer or cloth until it is almost dry before stencilling in the tulips. Leave to dry.

6 Paint the leaves in light green stencil paint with darker green shading. Paint the stems in dark green using an artist's paintbrush. Leave to dry.

7 Stencil the basket in pale brown stencil paint using a chunky stencil brush.

8 Stencil a single heart between each two baskets of tulips using red stencil paint.

Below: Make a matching key cupboard following the same method and using just one motif.

Above: A stencilled motif on a functional kitchen storage tin gives instant folk-art style.

FRENCH COUNTRY KITCHEN

This curtain design is adapted from the pattern on a French Art Deco soup bowl found in a fleamarket in Brussels. The flower design is also echoed in the hand-stencilled tiles and teams perfectly with the simple chequerboard border for a country look.

YOU WILL NEED

FOR THE CURTAIN:

white muslin (see measuring up)
iron
newspaper
masking tape
stencil card
craft knife and cutting mat
spray adhesive
solid stencil paint in blue
stencil brush
pressing cloth
needle
white sewing cotton
tape measure
dressmaker's chalk
white cotton tape
small pearl buttons

FOR THE TILES:

10 cm/4 in square white tiles
spray paint in red

MEASURING UP

To calculate the amount of muslin, allow 1.5 x the width of the window plus 2.5 cm/1 in for each side hem, and add 7.5 cm/3 in to the length for hems.

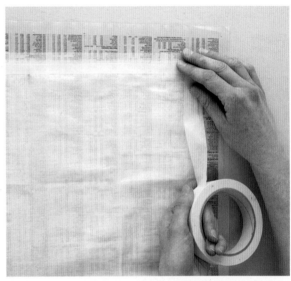

1 Press the muslin to remove any creases, then fold it lengthways in concertina folds. Press lightly to mark the creases, then fold it widthways in concertina folds and press again. These squares will act as a guide for positioning the motifs. Cover the work surface with newspaper and tape down the muslin so that it is taut.

2 Trace the three floral templates and the border template at the back of the book and cut out the stencils from stencil card as described in the basic techniques. Spray the back of one stencil with adhesive and, starting at the top right, lightly stencil the first motif.

3 Alternating the stencils as you work, stencil flowers in every other square over the whole curtain, leaving 15 cm/6 in free at the lower edge.

4 Stencil the blue chequerboard border along the bottom, lining up the stencil each time by matching the last two squares of the previous motif with the first two of the next stencil. Press the fabric well using a pressing cloth and iron.

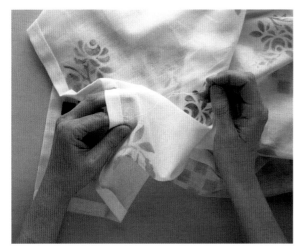

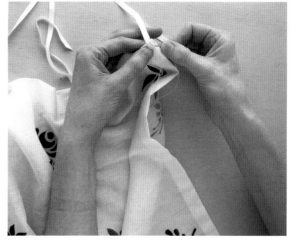

5 Press under and slip-stitch a 1.25 cm/½ in double hem around the sides and lower edge. Make a 2.5 cm/1 in double hem along the top edge.

6 Measure the top edge of the curtain and, using dressmakers' chalk, mark it into sections about 20 cm/8 in apart. Cut a 25 cm/10 in piece of cotton tape for each mark. Fold the first piece of tape in half and stitch to the back of the first mark. Sew a button on to the front of the curtain to anchor the tape. Repeat all the way along the edge and then tie the finished curtain on to the curtain pole in bows. ▶

Above: The simple tape ties that attach the curtain to the pole make an attractively rustic finish.

7 For the tiles, cut a piece of stencil card to fit the tile. Cut out the three floral stencils as before, using a craft knife and a cutting mat.

8 Cover the work-surface with newspaper. Using red spray paint, spray over the stencil lightly and evenly. Leave to dry, then remove the stencil.

Above: The coordinating tiles can be used individually as pot stands or set in the wall among plain white tiles.

TRAY OF AUTUMN LEAVES

The rich colours of autumn leaves are captured here on a simple wooden tray. Keep to warm natural paint colours to suit the country style and simple lines of the tray. Use the templates provided here or draw around your own pressed leaves.

YOU WILL NEED
wooden tray
fine-grade sandpaper
water-based primer (if bare wood)
emulsion paints in blue-grey and ochre
paintbrushes
household candle
cloth
stencil card
craft knife and cutting mat
spray adhesive
stencil brush
stencil paints in rust and terracotta
saucer
matt acrylic varnish

1 Sand down the tray with fine-grade sandpaper to ensure a smooth surface. If the wood is bare, paint with a water-based primer. Apply two coats of blue-grey paint, leaving it to dry between coats.

2 Rub the candle over the edges of the tray and over the base until there is a build-up of wax. Think about which areas of the tray would become worn naturally and apply wax there.

3 Wipe away any loose bits of wax. Paint the whole tray with the ochre paint and leave to dry completely.

▶

39

4 Lightly rub over the tray with sandpaper to reveal some of the blue-grey paint underneath.

5 Trace the templates at the back of the book or draw around pressed leaves. Cut out the stencils from stencil card as described in the basic techniques.

Above: Building up layers of paint and rubbing back the top layer in places gives the tray a pleasing distressed look.

6 Lightly spray the back of the stencils with adhesive. Arrange the stencils on the tray and smooth down. Dip the stencil brush into the rust stencil paint and rub it on a saucer or cloth so that the brush is dry. Using circular movements, apply the colour evenly over the stencils, working more on one side of each motif. Apply terracotta paint to the other side of the leaves to give shadow. Continue stencilling all over the tray. To give the tray a tough finish, apply two or three coats of varnish, leaving each coat to dry before applying the next.

GILDED CANDLES

Plain church candles look extra special when adorned with simple gold stars and stripes. Always associated with Christmas, candles are popular all year round for their soft romantic lighting. Cutting the stencils may be fiddly but it is then a quick job to spray on the gold paint.

YOU WILL NEED
acetate
selection of candles
marker pen
craft knife and cutting mat
spray adhesive
masking tape
metallic spray paint

1 Wrap a piece of acetate around the candle. Mark and cut it to fit exactly. Do not over-lap the edges. Cut it a few mil-limetres shorter than the candle.

2 Trace the star templates at the back of the book. Lay a piece of acetate over the stars and trace over them with a marker pen.

3 Cut out the stars using a craft knife and cutting mat. Be careful not to tear the acetate.

4 Spray one side of the stencil with adhesive and wrap around the candle, centring it so that there is a small gap at either end. Secure the acetate join with masking tape. Mask the top of the candle with tape, ensuring there are no gaps.

▶

5 Spray a fine mist of metallic spray paint over the candle, holding the can about 30 cm/ 12 in from the surface. If too much paint is applied, it will drip underneath the stencil. Keep checking that the stencil is well stuck down to avoid any fuzzy lines around the stars. Leave the paint to dry for a couple of minutes, then carefully remove the masking tape and acetate.

6 For a stars and stripes candle, cut strips of acetate and trace a line of small stars along each strip. Cut out with a craft knife as before. Spray one side of the acetate strips with adhesive. Stick the strips on to the candle, measuring the gaps in between to ensure equal spacing. Secure them with small pieces of masking tape at the join.

7 Mask off the top of the candle as before. Spray the candle with metallic paint and remove the masking tape and stencil when dry.

8 For a reverse stencil design, cut out individual star shapes from acetate. Apply spray adhesive to one side, stick on to the candle and mask off the top of the candle as before. Spray with metallic paint and carefully remove the acetate stars when the paint is dry.

Above: A basketful of starry gilded candles makes a pretty gift.

RENAISSANCE ART

Turn your hallway into a dramatic entrance with ornate stencils and rich colours. Combine them with gold accessories, velvets and braids to complete the theatrical setting. This design would also be ideal for creating an intimate dining room for candlelit dinners.

YOU WILL NEED
ruler
spirit level
pencil
masking tape
emulsion paints in pale slate-blue, terracotta
and pale peach
sponges
stencil brushes
stencil card
craft knife and cutting mat
stencil paints in dark grey-blue, terracotta,
emerald and turquoise

1 Using a ruler and spirit level, divide the wall in half horizontally with a pencil line, then draw a second line 15 cm/6 in above the first. Stick a line of masking tape just below this top line. Dilute one part slate-blue emulsion with one part water and colour the top half of the wall using a sponge.

2 Stick masking tape just above the bottom pencil line. Dilute terracotta emulsion with water and sponge over the lower half of the wall.

3 Sponge lightly over the terracotta with slate-blue to add a textural effect. Remove the strips of masking tape.

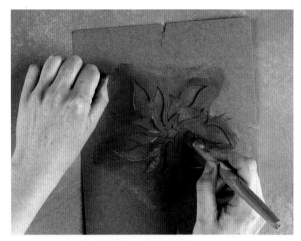

4 Colour the centre band with diluted peach emulsion using a stencil brush. Trace the templates at the back of the book and cut out the stencils from stencil card.

5 Stencil the wall motifs at roughly regular intervals over the upper part of the wall, using dark grey-blue. Rotate the stencil with every alternate motif to give movement to the design.

6 Starting at the right-hand side of the peach band, stencil the border motif with terracotta stencil paint. Add details in emerald and turquoise. Continue along the wall, positioning the stencil beside the previous motif so that the spaces are equal.

Right: Make a matching patchwork cushion cover with pieces of fabric stencilled with gold fabric paint. Add offcuts of velvet and cover all the seams with ornate trimmings.

GEOMETRIC FLOOR TILES

This repeating pattern is derived from an ancient Greek mosaic floor. Cork floor tiles take colour well - only use a small amount of paint and build it up in layers if necessary. Make two stencils, one for each colour, so that the colours do not get mixed.

YOU WILL NEED
graph paper
ruler
pencil
compass
stencil card
craft knife and cutting mat
masking tape
30 cm /12 in cork tiles
spray adhesive
stencil paints in terracotta and blue
stencil brushes
acrylic sealer

1 Enlarge the quarter section template at the back of the book so that it will fit within a 15 cm/ 6 in square. Using graph paper will make the design more accurate. Rule the three squares and draw the curves with a compass. Rub over all the pencil lines on the back with a pencil.

2 Cut two 30 cm/12 in squares from stencil card and draw four lines, from corner to corner and edge to edge, to divide each card into eight equal segments. For the first stencil, tape the paper face up to one corner of the first card and draw around the corner and centre square to transfer the design to the card. Repeat on each corner, turning the paper 90° each time. Cut out the five squares. For the second stencil, draw along the curves and around the remaining square. Cut out these eight shapes.

3 Wipe the tile to remove any cork dust and coat the back of the first stencil with spray adhesive. Stencil the squares using terracotta stencil paint and a stencil brush.

4 Leave to dry, then use the second stencil and blue paint to complete the design. Stencil the remaining tiles in the same way.

5 When all the tiles are complete, spray with acrylic sealer to make them waterproof. Fix them to the floor following the manufacturer's instructions.

Above: Make half the tiles in different colours to make a chequerboard-patterned floor.

Right: A gentle shading of blue has been added to the yellow shapes and yellow to the blue shapes to give a softer outline to the design.

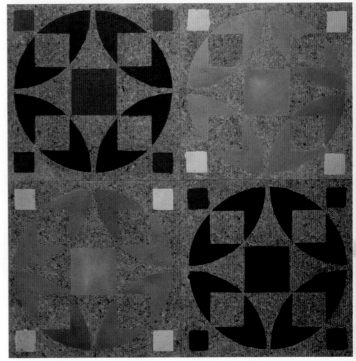

Right: Different colour combinations create quite different effects. When using more than two colours, you will either need to cut more stencils or to mask out the area that will be coloured differently.

ORGANZA CUSHION

If you always thought stencilling had a simple country look, then think again. This brilliant organza cushion with gold stencilling takes the craft into the luxury class. Use the sharpest dressmaker's pins when handling organza to avoid marking the fabric.

YOU WILL NEED
dressmaker's graph paper
ruler
pencil
scissors
dressmaker's pins
organza, 1 m/1⅛ yd each in main colour and contrast colour
stencil card
craft knife and cutting mat
spray adhesive
scrap paper
masking tape
gold spray paint
needle and thread
sewing machine
iron
50 cm/20 in cushion pad

1 Copy the border template at the back of the book on to dressmaker's graph paper and cut it out. In addition, cut out a 53 cm/21 in square and a 53 x 40 cm/21 x 16 in rectangle from graph paper.

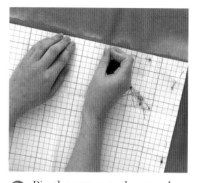

2 Pin the square and rectangle to the main colour organza. Cut two 53 cm /21 in squares, and two rectangles measuring 53 x 40 cm/21 x 16 in from the main fabric. Cut four border pieces from the contrasting fabric.

3 Cut a piece of stencil card 18 x 53 cm/7 x 21 in. Trace the template and transfer to the card, 8 cm/3 in from the bottom edge and with 6 cm/ 2½ in to spare at each end. Cut out the stencil.

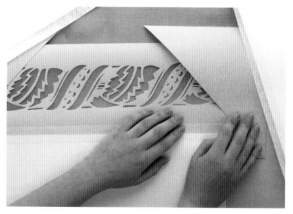

4 Spray the back of the stencil with adhesive and position along the edge of the main organza fabric square. Cut two 45° mitres from stencil card, spray with adhesive and press in place. Mask off the surrounding areas with scrap paper. ▶

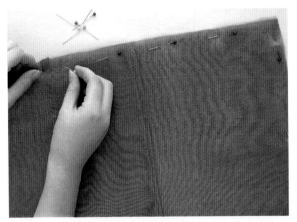

5 Spray with gold paint. Leave to dry and spray again. Remove the masking paper and stencil. Place the stencil along the next edge, put the mitres in place and continue as before. Stencil the remaining two sides. Hem one long edge of each fabric rectangle by folding over 1 cm/⅜ in, then 1.5 cm/⅝ in. Pin, tack and machine stitch the hem, then press.

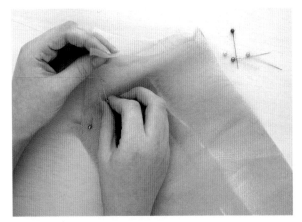

6 Lay the stencilled fabric square face down and the second square on top. Lay the two rectangles on top of these, overlapping the stitched edges so that the raw edges line up with the square pieces. Pin, tack and machine stitch 1 cm/⅜ in from the raw edge. Trim seam allowance to 7 mm/¼ in. Pin, tack and stitch the border pieces together at the mitred corners 1.3 cm/½ in from the raw edges. Trim the corners and turn the right way out. Press. Continue until the border pieces make a ring.

7 Press one of the raw edges under by 1.3 cm/ ½ in. Lay the pressed edge of the border fabric along the edge of the main fabric square and pin, tack and stitch in place.

8 Turn the cushion over and pull the border over. Turn under the border's raw edge by 1.3 cm/½ in and pin in place along the front of the cushion. Tack and stitch in place. Press. Insert the cushion pad.

TABLECLOTH AND NAPKINS

Inspiration for stencil designs can be all around you, waiting to be discovered. Cutlery and kitchen utensils are wonderful graphic shapes, ideal for stencilling. Arrange them as borders around the edge of a cloth or place them formally on each side of an imaginary place setting.

YOU WILL NEED
acetate
craft knife and cutting mat
plain-coloured cotton napkins
and tablecloth
fabric paints in various colours
stencil brush
fine artist's paintbrush
iron

1 Trace the cutlery, heart and utensils templates at the back of the book and cut the stencils from acetate. Lay one of the napkins on a flat surface. Plan your design and start to stencil around the edge of the napkin.

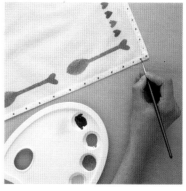

2 Stencil hearts in between the cutlery stencils. Using a fine artist's paintbrush, paint dots around the hem of the napkins.

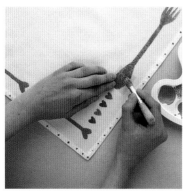

3 With the stencil brush stencil hearts on the handles of some of the cutlery.

4 Stencil each napkin with a different pattern, varying the arrangement of the stencils.

5 Lay the tablecloth on a flat surface and begin to stencil the border of cutlery and hearts.

▶

6 Stencil the larger utensil shapes in the middle of the tablecloth. Stencil the handles first. Paint the top of the utensils, for example the whisk, in a contrasting colour.

7 Stencil the draining spoons and then add the draining holes in a different colour.

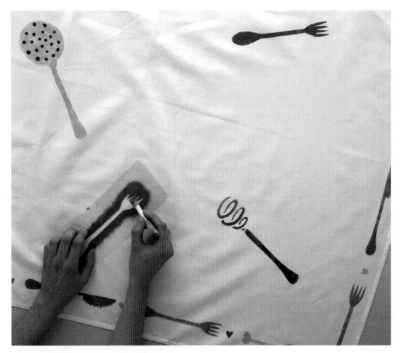

8 Fill in the areas around the utensils with more cutlery stencils. Leave the fabric paint to dry and then iron the reverse of the fabric to fix the paint.

THROUGH THE GRAPEVINE

This classic grape stencil will bring back holiday memories of sipping Greek wine under a canopy of vines. The stencilled grapes are all the more effective set against the purple and green dry-brushed walls. Practise your paint effects on small boards before tackling full-scale walls.

YOU WILL NEED
large paintbrush
emulsion paints in purple and green
pencil
ruler
spirit level
acetate
craft knife and cutting mat
masking tape
stencil paint in purple and lilac
stencil brush
silver gilt cream
soft cloth

1 Dip the end of a large paintbrush in purple emulsion, scrape off the excess and apply to the wall, brushing in varying directions and not completely covering the wall. This process is known as dry-brushing.

2 Repeat the process with green emulsion, filling in some of the gaps.

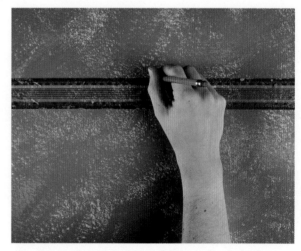

3 Draw a horizontal pencil line at the desired height on the wall using a ruler and spirit level.

4 Trace the grape stencil at the back of the book and cut the stencil from acetate. Tape the stencil in place with its top edge on the pencil line. Apply purple stencil paint over the whole stencil.

5 Add lilac stencil paint at the bottom of each window in the stencil to create highlights.

6 Dip the stencil brush in the silver gilt cream, brush off any excess and brush over the design using an up and down movement.

7 Select a few leaf shapes from the stencil and mask off. Position randomly over the wall and stencil in purple. Brush over with the gilt cream. (They are too small to require the lilac highlight.)

▶

8 Leave the stencilling to dry overnight. With a soft cloth, buff up the silver cream to a shine.

ROPE AND SHELLS

The chunky rope cleverly linking the seashells is echoed by individual stencilled knots. Shells are always popular motifs for a bathroom design and look good in many colour combinations, from nautical blue and white to greens and aquas or pinks and corals.

YOU WILL NEED
large household sponges
emulsion paints in nautical blue and white
ruler
spirit level
pencil
acetate
craft knife and cutting mat
masking tape
stencil paints in dark blue, light blue and camel
stencil brush
rubber
cloth

1 Using a household sponge rub nautical blue emulsion paint over the wall to create a very rough and patchy finish. Leave to dry.

2 Using a clean sponge, rub a generous amount of white emulsion over the wall so that it almost covers the blue, giving a slightly mottled effect.

3 Using a ruler and spirit level, draw a horizontal pencil line at the desired height of the border. Trace the seashore and knot templates at the back of the book and cut the stencils from acetate. Position the seashore stencil with its top edge on the pencil line and secure with masking tape. Stencil dark blue paint around the edges of the shells and seaweed, using a stencil brush.

4 Using light blue stencil paint, shade in the shells, the seaweed and the recesses of the rope.

5 Using the camel stencil paint, fill in the remainder of the rope and highlight the shells and seaweed. Continue to stencil the shell and rope border right around the room.

6 Draw a vertical line from each loop of rope to the skirting board. Starting 30 cm/12 in from the border, make pencil marks at 30cm/12 in intervals down the line to mark the positions of the knots. Start every alternate line of marks 15 cm/6 in below the border so that the knots will be staggered. ▶

7 Tape the knotted rope stencil on to the first pencil mark. Stencil dark blue in the recesses of the rope.

8 Stencil the remainder of the rope in camel. Leave to dry. Remove any visible pencil marks with a rubber and wipe over with a slightly damp cloth.

Left: Create a variation on the sea theme by stencilling a row of starfish at dado-rail height.

HERALDIC DINING ROOM

Lend an atmosphere of medieval luxury to your dining room with richly coloured walls and heraldic motifs stencilled in the same deep tones. Gilt accessories, heavy fabrics and a profusion of candles team well with this decor. All that remains is to prepare a sumptuous banquet.

YOU WILL NEED
large household sponges
emulsion paints in camel, deep red and deep purple
ruler
spirit level
pencil
masking tape
acetate
craft knife and cutting mat
stencil brush
fine lining brush

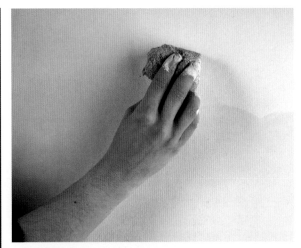

1 Using a large household sponge, rub camel emulsion all over the wall. Leave to dry.

2 Repeat the process using a generous amount of deep red emulsion so that it almost covers the camel, giving a slightly mottled effect. Leave to dry.

3 Using a ruler and spirit level, draw a pencil line at dado-rail height and stick a line of masking tape just above it.

66

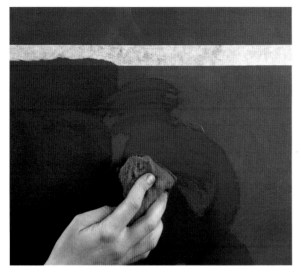

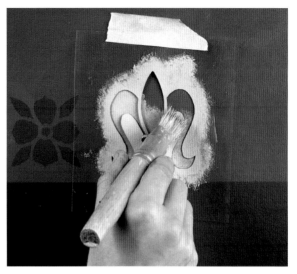

4 Sponge deep purple emulsion all over the wall below the masking tape to give a slightly mottled effect. Leave to dry, then remove the masking tape.

5 Trace the heraldic templates at the back of the book and cut the stencils from acetate. Secure the rose stencil above the dividing line and stencil in purple emulsion, using the stencil brush. When dry, position the fleur-de-lys stencil next to the rose and stencil in camel emulsion. Continue to alternate the stencils around the room.

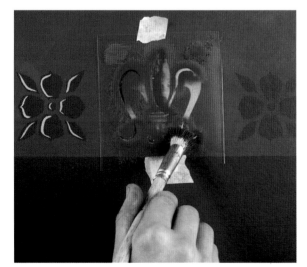

6 Place the highlighting stencils over the painted motifs and, with a stencil brush, add purple highlights to the camel fleurs-de-lys and camel highlights to the purple roses.

7 Flip the stencils over and position as mirror images below the previously stencilled motifs. Stencil the roses in camel and the fleurs-de-lys in red. ▶

8 Add highlights as before, using camel on the fleurs-de-lys and purple on the camel roses.

9 Using a fine lining brush and camel paint, paint a narrow line where the red and purple paints meet. If you do not have the confidence to do this freehand, position two rows of masking tape on the wall, leaving a small gap in between. When the line of paint is dry, carefully remove the masking tape.

TROMPE-L'ŒIL PLATES

A shelf full of decorative painted plates adds a witty touch to a kitchen corner. Follow these plate designs or translate your own patterned china into stencils to give a co-ordinated look. Why not add some individual plates to the wall as well?

YOU WILL NEED
stencil card
pencil
ruler
craft knife and cutting mat
23 cm/9 in diameter plate
compass
spray adhesive
newspaper or brown paper
masking tape
spray paints in white, cream, a
range of pinks and mauves, light
green, dark green, red, blue and grey

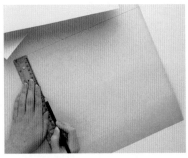

1 Cut three pieces of stencil card 30 cm/12 in square. Mark the centre of each card by measuring the centre of each edge and ruling a horizontal and a vertical line across each card to join the marks.

2 Draw a line 3.5 cm/1¼ in in from all four edges of each card. Place the plate in the centre of the card and draw around the edge. Cut out the plate shape from the first piece of stencil card (stencil 1).

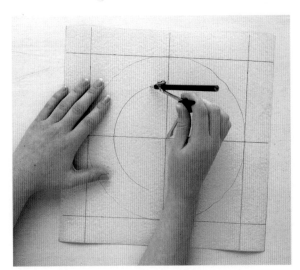

3 Using a compass, draw a circle about 4 cm/ 1 ½ in from the edge of the plate on the two remaining pieces of card.

4 Trace or photocopy the plate template at the back of the book to the desired size and transfer to the second stencil card.

5 Cut out the design with a craft knife on a cutting mat. Cut out the smaller areas first and the larger areas last (stencil 2). On the third piece of stencil card, cut out the inner circle (stencil 3).

6 Draw a faint horizontal pencil line on the wall and put two marks 30 cm/12 in apart on the line to act as a guide for positioning the stencils. Spray the back of the plate stencil (1) with adhesive and place in position on the wall. Press down firmly to ensure a good contact. Mask off the surrounding area with paper and masking tape, leaving no gaps. Spray white and cream spray paint on to the stencil. Remove the masks and stencil.

7 Attach the flower stencil (2) to the wall with spray adhesive, lining it up with the marks on the wall. Mask off the surrounding area. Stick small pieces of masking tape over the leaves on the stencil. Spray the flowers with pinks and mauves, applying a fine layer of paint in short sharp puffs. Try each paint colour on the mask surrounding the stencil to test the colour and to make sure that the nozzle is clear.

8 Remove the masking tape from the leaves. Fold a small piece of card in half and use it to shield the rest of the stencil from paint. Spray the leaves using light and dark green paints, trying not to get too much green on the flowers.

9 Cut a small hole in a piece of card and use to spray the centres of the flowers green.

10 Hold the shield of card around the dot designs on the border, and spray each one with red paint. Spray blue paint over the wavy lines on the border. Again, do not apply too much paint. Remove the masks and carefully remove the stencil. ▶

11 Spray the back of the last stencil (3) with adhesive and position on the wall. Mask off the surrounding area as before. Spray an extremely fine mist of grey paint over the top left-hand side and bottom right-hand side of the plate design to create a shadow. Aim the nozzle slightly away from the stencil to ensure that hardly any paint hits the wall. Remove the masks and stencil.

12 Reposition stencil 1 on the wall and spray a very fine mist of blue paint around the edge of the plate. Repeat all stages along the edge of the shelf length.

CELESTIAL CHERUBS

This exuberant baroque decoration is perfect for a sumptuous bedroom.
The cherubs are stencilled in metallic shades of bronze, gold and copper, but you could use
plain colours for a simpler result that would be suitable for a child's room.

YOU WILL NEED
emulsion paints in white, blue and grey
paintbrush
sponge
stencil card
craft knife and cutting mat
masking tape
stencil paints in gold, copper, bronze and white
stencil brush

1 Paint the wall with white emulsion. Next, dilute one part blue emulsion with one part water, and, using a sponge, lightly apply it to the wall.

2 Sponge in a few areas of grey to give the impression of a cloudy sky. Sponge in a few pale areas by mixing a little white into the grey paint to suggest the edges of clouds.

3 Trace the cherub and heart templates at the back of the book and cut the stencils from stencil card. Secure the cherub stencil to the wall with masking tape. Stencil the body of the cherub in gold.

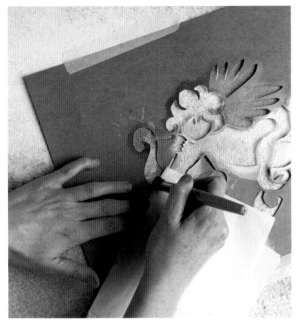

4 Stencil the wings and bow in copper, covering the adjacent parts of the stencil with scrap paper.

5 Stencil the hair and arrow in bronze.

6 Stencil the drape in white with some bronze shadows.

7 To give a three-dimensional effect to the whole design, add bronze shadows at the edges of the various parts of the motif.

8 Stencil more cherubs, varying the design by reversing the card sometimes. Stencil the interlinked hearts in the spaces using bronze paint.

Right: Try to position the stencils so that the cupids are aiming their arrows at the interlinked hearts – perfect for a romantic bedroom.

MATERIALS

A variety of materials can be used for stencilling, from specialist stencilling paints and sticks to acrylics and emulsion. Each has its own properties and will create different effects.

ACRYLIC STENCIL PAINTS

Acrylic stencil paint is quick-drying, reducing the chance of the paint running and seaping behind the stencil. Acrylic stencil paints are available in a wide range of colours and can be mixed for more subtle shades.

ACRYLIC VARNISH

This is useful for sealing finished projects.

EMULSION PAINTS

Ordinary household emulsion can also be used for stencilling. It is best to avoid the cheaper varieties as these contain alot of water and will seap through the stencil.

FABRIC PAINTS

These are used in the same way as acrylic stencil paints, and come in an equally wide range of colours. Fixed with an iron according to the manufacturer's instructions, they will withstand washing and everyday use. As with ordinary stencil paint do not overload the brush with colour, as it will seap into the fabric. Always back the fabric you are stencilling with scrap paper or newspaper to prevent the paints from marking the work surface.

GOLD LEAF AND GOLD SIZE

These can be used to spectacular effect. The actual design is stencilled with gold size. The size is then left to become tacky and the gold leaf rubbed over the design.

METALLIC CREAMS

These are available in many different metallic finishes, from gold through to bronze and copper and silver. Apply as highlights on a painted base, or use for the entire design. Creams can be applied with cloths or your fingertip.

OIL-BASED STENCIL STICKS AND CREAMS

The sticks can be used in the same way as a wax crayon, while the creams can be applied with a brush or your fingertip. With either one, there is no danger of overloading the colour, and they won't run. The disadvantage is their long drying time (overnight in some cases); also, the colours can become muddy when mixed. Sticks and creams are also available for fabrics.

Clockwise from top left: acrylic stencil paints, oil-based cream and metallic creams, fabric paints, oil-based stencil sticks, emulsion paints, gold leaf, acrylic varnish and gold size.

EQUIPMENT

Stencilling does not require a great deal of specialist equipment; many of the items used are commonly found in most households. Some items, however, will make the job easier.

BRUSHES

It is worth investing in a set of good stencil brushes. The ends of the brushes should be flat and the bristles firm, to allow you to control the application of paint. A medium-sized brush (1½ in/3 cm diameter) is a useful, all-purpose size, but you may want to buy one size smaller and one size larger as well. You will need a selection of household paintbrushes for applying large areas of background colour, and small artist's paintbrushes for adding fine details.

CRAFT KNIFE OR SCALPEL

Use either for cutting out stencils from card.

CUTTING MAT

This provides a firm surface to cut into and will help prevent the craft knife or scalpel from slipping.

MASKING TAPE

As the stencil may need to be repositioned it is advisable to hold it in place with masking tape, which can be removed fairly easily from most surfaces.

PAINT-MIXING CONTAINER

This may be necessary for mixing paints and colourwashes.

PENCILS

Keep a selection of soft and hard pencils to transfer the stencil design on to card. Use an ordinary pencil to mark the positions of the stencils before applying.

STENCIL CARD

The material used to make the stencil is a matter of preference. Specialty stencil card is available waxed, which means that it will last longer, but ordinary card or heavy paper can also be used. It is worth purchasing a sheet of clear acetate if you wish to keep your stencil design, to reuse time and again.

TAPE MEASURE AND STRAIGHT-EDGES

Some patterns may require accuracy. Measuring and planning the positions of your stencils before you begin will aid the result.

TRACING PAPER

Use to trace and transfer your stencil design on to stencil card.

Clockwise from top left: straight-edges, tape measure, stencil brushes, household paintbrush, cutting mat, stencil card, tracing paper, soft pencil, scalpel, paint-mixing container, masking tape.

BASIC TECHNIQUES

Stencilling is not difficult to master, but it is worth practising on a small area to get used to han-dling the brush and to become accustomed to the properties of the paints you use. Some of the tips and techniques suggested below will make the task easier.

TRANSFERRING TEMPLATES

1 To transfer a template on to a piece of stencil card, place a piece of tracing paper over the design, and draw over it with a hard pencil.

2 Turn over the tracing paper, and on the back of the design rub over the lines you have drawn with a soft pencil.

3 Turn the tracing paper back to the right side and place on top of a sheet of stencil card. Draw over the original lines with a hard pencil.

CUTTING STENCILS

1 Place the stencil on to a cutting mat or piece of thick cardboard and tape in place. Use a craft knife or scalpel for cutting.

2 It is safer to move the cutting board towards you and the knife when working round awk-ward shapes. Continue, moving the board as necessary.

BLOCK STENCILLING

Use for filling in large areas in a single, solid colour. As in all stencilling, remember not to apply the paint too heavily – less is more. Always blot out the paint on to a piece of blotting card before you begin.

BLOCK STENCILLING WITH SECOND COLOUR STIPPLED

When applying two colours, always apply the lighter shade first, then the darker. Do not cover the entire surface with the first colour; leave a gap for the second shade, then blend later. Use a separate, clean brush for each colour.

TWO-COLOUR BLOCKING

When you apply the first colour, do not fully block out the petals; instead, outline them with the first colour and leave the centres bare. Use the second colour to fill. Take care not to apply your paint too heavily.

ROTATED FLOWER WITH BLOCKED LEAVES

Using a very dry brush with a tiny amount of paint, rotate the bristles in a circular motion. This rotating action leaves enough paint on the surface for a lighter, softer look than a block application. Use the same effect in a darker colour on the inside of the petals.

ROTATING AND SHADING

Using a very dry brush with a tiny amount of paint, place your brush on one side of the stencil and rotate the brush in circles. Repeat, using a slightly darker colour on the edges, for soft shading.

ROTATING AND SHADING IN TWO COLOURS

This is similar to rotating and shading, but is more directional. Using a very dry brush with a tiny amount of paint, place your brush in the centre of the flower and rotate the bristles slightly outwards. Repeat, using a slightly darker colour.

ROTATING BRUSH WITH LEAVES FLICKED

Fill in the petals by rotating a very dry brush and a tiny amount of paint. For the flicking effect on the leaves, use slightly more paint on the brush. Working from the centre, flick the paint outwards once or twice. Do not overdo.

DRY BRUSHING, ROTATING FROM EDGE

Using big circular strokes, work from the outside of the whole stencil, moving inwards. This should leave you with more paint on the outside, as there will be less and less paint on your brush as you move.

BRUSHING UP AND DOWN FROM SIDES

This is similar to flicking. Using slightly more paint on your brush than you would for rotating, brush up and down, then from side to side. Keep your lines vertical and horizontal to give a lined effect.

BRUSHING UP AND DOWN

Using slightly more paint on your brush than you would for rotating, brush up and down only, taking care to keep your lines vertical.

DRY BRUSHING WITH CURVE

Using the rotating technique, start at the centre and work outwards in big circles.

DRY BRUSHING AND ROTATING

Apply a tiny amount of paint by rotating the bristles from the centre, and from the outside tips, to give more paint in these areas. Work along the line, using less pressure than on the centre and the tips. This gives a softer effect on the areas in between.

ROUGH STIPPLING

This method uses more paint and less pressure than rotating or flicking. Taking a reasonable amount of paint on the bristles of your brush, simply place it down lightly. This gives a rougher look. Do not go over it too many times as this spoils the effect.

DRY BRUSH STIPPLING

This is similar to stippling, except that it is essential to dab most of the paint off the bristles before you start. This gives a softer stippling effect.

TWO-COLOUR STIPPLING

Use less paint than for rough stippling. The second colour is stippled out from the centre, to blend.

GENTLE STIPPLING FROM EDGE

Using a very dry brush (dab most of the paint off the bristles before you start), stipple from the outside, working inwards. By the time you get to the centre, there should be hardly any paint left on your brush, ensuring a very soft paint effect in this area.

ONE-SIDED STIPPLING

Apply the lighter colour first, up to a point just past the centre. Apply the darker colour, and stipple to the centre. Always start on the outer edge so that you leave more paint on the edges of the stencil design.

STIPPLING TO SHADE WITH
TWO COLOURS

Using a reasonable amount of paint, apply the lighter shade first. Apply the darker shade to one side only of each window. (Here, the second colour is applied to the right-hand side). A few dabs of the darker colour paint is quite sufficient.

FLICKING UPWARD WITH BRUSH

Using a reasonable amount of paint (not too wet or too dry) on your brush, flick upwards only. This creates a line at the top of the petals and leaves.

FLICKING IN TWO DIRECTIONS

Using a reasonable amount of paint on your brush, flick up and down. Do not use too much paint as it will collect on the edges.

FLICKING FROM THE OUTSIDE TO THE CENTRE

Using a reasonable amount of paint on your brush, flick from the outside edges in to the centre of the design. Flick from the top to the centre, from the bottom to the centre, from the left to the centre, and from the right to the centre.

FLICKING FROM THE TOP TO THE CENTRE

Using a reasonable amount of paint, flick from the top edge of the window to the centre of the design, then from the bottom edge to the centre.

RIGHT-HAND DROP SHADOW

Apply the first colour, which should be your lighter shade, using a block effect. Concentrate on one side of each window (here, the right-hand side). Move the stencil slightly to the left – a few millimetres is sufficient – taking care to not move it up or down. Block again, using a darker colour.

TEMPLATES

Enlarge the templates on a photocopier, or trace the design and draw a grid of evenly spaced squares over your tracing. Draw a larger grid on to another piece of paper and copy the outline square by square. Draw over the lines to make sure they are continuous.

Frosted Vases, pp 8-10. Scale up.

Art Nouveau Hatbox pp 15-16. Scale up.

Star Picture Frames pp 17-19. Same size.

Making Sandcastles pp 20-3. Scale up.

Seashore Bathroom Set pp 25-6.
Same size.

Greek Urns pp 27-9. Same size.

89

*French Country
Kitchen pp 34-7.
Same size.*

*Tray of Autumn
Leaves pp 38-
40. Same size.*

*Pennsylvania-Dutch Tulips
pp30-3. Same size.*

90

Gilded Candles pp 41-3.
Same size.

Heraldic Dining
Room pp 66-69.
Scale up.

Renaissance
Art pp 44-7.
Scale up.

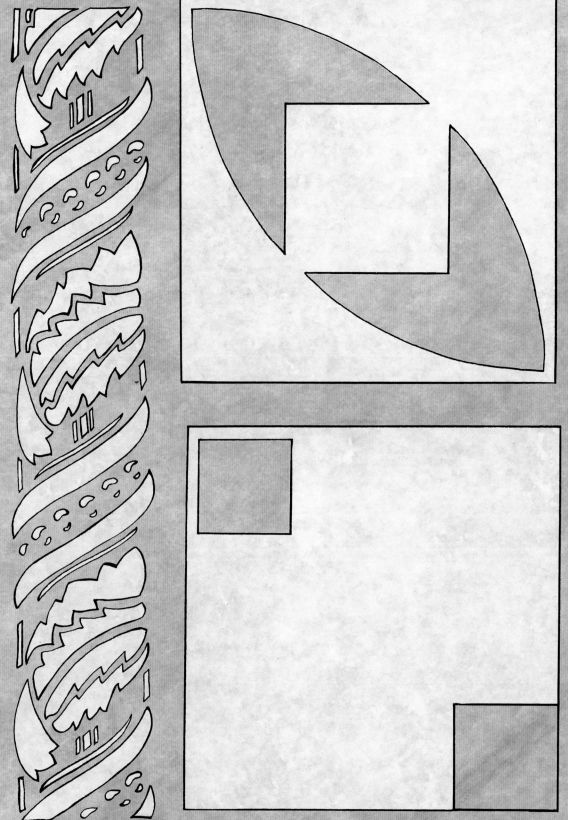

Geometr
Floor Ti
pp 48-5
Scale up.

Organza
Cushion
pp 52-4.
Scale up.

*Through the
Grapevine pp
58-61. Scale up.*

*Tablecloth
and Napkins
pp 55-7.
Scale up.*

Celestial Cherubs
pp 74-7. Scale up.

Rope a
Shells
pp 62-
Scale u

Trompe-l'œil Plates
pp 70-3. Scale up.

SUPPLIERS

The specialist materials and equipment that you will require for the stencilling projects featured in this book are available from any good art supply shop.

Cornelissen & Son Ltd
105 Great Russell Street
London WC1B 3RY

Crown Paints
Crown Decorative Products Ltd
PO Box 37
Crown House
Hollins Road
Darwen
Lancashire BB3 0BG

Daler-Rowney Ltd
PO Box 10
Southern Industrial Estate
Bracknell
Berkshire RG12 8ST

London Graphic Centre
16 Shelton Street
London WC2H 9JJ
Specialist art supplies

Paint Magic
79 Shepperton Road
Islington
London N1 3DF

E. Ploton Ltd
273 Archway Road
London N6 5AA
Art and gilding materials

Russell & Chapple Ltd
23 Monmouth Street
London WC2H 9DE

Stuart Stephenson Ltd
68 Clerkenwell Road
London EC1M 5QA
Art and gilding materials

Winsor & Newton
Whitefriars Avenue
Wealdstone
Harrow
Middlesex HA3 5RH

ACKNOWLEDGEMENTS

The publishers would like to thank the following people for designing the projects in this book: Sacha Cohen for the Greek Urns pp 27-9, Through the Grapevine pp 58-61, Rope and Shells pp 62-5, Heraldic Dining Room pp 66-9; Petra Boase for the Frosted Vases pp 8-10, Painted Drawers pp 11-13, Star Frame pp 17-19, Making Sandcastles pp 20-3, Seashore Bathroom set pp 24-6, Tablecloth and Napkins pp 55-7; Lucinda Ganderton for the Art Nouveau Hatbox pp 14-16, Pennsylvania-Dutch Tulips pp 30-3, French Country Kitchen pp 34-7, Renaissance Art pp 44-7, Geometric Floor Tiles pp 48-51, Celestial Cherubs pp 74-7; Emma Hardy for the Tray of Autumn Leaves pp 38-40, Gilded Candles pp 41-3, Organza Cushion pp 52-4, Trompe-l'œil Plates pp 70-3.

INDEX